Blackwater Mine

Written by John Parsons

Illustrated by Trudi Canavan

Contents | Page

NELSON
THOMSON LEARNING

Blackwater Mine

With these characters ...

Young
Nat

Mister
Hodge

Charlie
Grimes

"A feeling of terror

Setting the scene ...

In 1820, which is the year this story begins, coal was the most powerful fuel the world knew. But mining the coal from deep below the ground was a dangerous job.

At Blackwater Mine, the coal miners work in dark, dangerous conditions. And the mine owner, Mr Hodge, doesn't want to spend money to make it safer. When Young Nat, his son, sneaks down the mine, both father and son discover just how deadly a mine can be!

gripped me for the first time."

Chapter 1.

Coal mining has always been dangerous. And, of all the coal mines in the country, Blackwater Mine was the most dangerous.

As a young boy, my thoughts were always on adventure, not danger. But one black night, my adventures led to a disaster that changed Blackwater Mine forever. Here, then, is my story ...

My name is Nathaniel Hodge. Even though I am over fifty years old now, most people still call me Young Nat. They call me Young Nat because they remember my father, whose name was also Nathaniel. But, in the old days, no-one ever dared call him anything but Mister Hodge.

My father was a very rich man. On the outskirts of our village was Blackwater Mine, where almost every man and his son worked. My father owned the coal mine. He was the most important man in the village.

Every morning, he would arrive at the mine in his horse-drawn carriage wearing his finest clothes. While he worked in his office, the miners worked in dark, grimy tunnels, hacking coal from deep underground. My father had no idea what it was like for his miners working in such dirty, dangerous conditions.

Coal powered the huge, hissing pump that removed water out of our mine, pumping bucket loads of black, coal-coloured water into the pond nearby. Ever since the pump was built, our coal mine had been known as Blackwater Mine. One look at the black, coal-coloured pond, and it was easy to tell why!

It hadn't been easy to convince my father to pay for the pump. Before it was built, the miners had to wade through deep, dark water that seeped into the tunnels deep below the surface. It was dirty, dangerous work, and the rising water was a constant threat to their lives.

"I can't afford a pump," my father would grumble from behind his huge desk. He would point at the accounts books in which he wrote down every penny he spent, and every penny the mine earned. "Already, I have to pay those men and boys far too much money. Every penny counts, you know!"

Who convinced my father! Well my mother of course!

When it came to money, my father had plenty of it. He had no trouble selling every lump of black coal that the miners hacked out of our mine with their picks and shovels. It was just that he hated to spend money.

"But it will be much safer for the miners if they don't have to work in damp, wet conditions," my mother would say.

"I can't afford to care about safety," my father would reply irritably. "If it will make my miners work faster, I will think about it."

When my father finally agreed to build the pump, it did allow the miners to work more quickly, of course. My father still grumbled, but as he saw the extra money adding up in his accounts books, he became less irritable.

Unfortunately, I wasn't allowed to play with the other children in the village. My father said that I should not be seen playing with the sons and daughters of poor miners. But I managed to sneak out whenever I could. My best friend, my secret friend, was Charlie Grimes.

Charlie's dad, Bert, worked every night in our mine as a fireman. Even though Charlie was only ten, he worked with his father, too.

Every day they would wait until all the miners had trudged, exhausted, back to their houses. I would watch from my window as night fell. Charlie and his father would walk by, whistling, to start their dangerous work.

When we first became friends, I would ask, "Why do you whistle?"

"Because, each night, we're just happy to be alive," Charlie would answer, as if it was a dumb question.

Secretly, I wished I could go with them, deep into the empty mine. I wished I could see what it was like, crouching and crawling through the black, dust-filled tunnels, with only a small, flickering oil lamp for guidance.

Charlie told me about the many dangers awaiting the miners deep below the surface. The tunnels might collapse, leaving them trapped. The pump might stop working, making the water rise rapidly. The worst danger that Charlie described was one that every miner feared — the threat of an explosion.

It was Charlie and his dad's job to prevent explosions. Deep in the mine's tunnels, dangerous gases swirled unseen. Together with the coal dust hanging in the air, they made a deadly mix. The tiny flame of the miner's oil lamp could set off an enormous explosion. With his dad, Charlie checked for dangerous gases every night.

Whenever Charlie explained their job I was fascinated by how brave they were. The black coal dust around his cheeks and forehead always seemed to make him look older and wiser than his age. And when he lowered his voice, his explanation made my skin shiver.

"It works like this. We crawl along on our hands and knees, deeper and deeper into the tunnels. My father carries his fireman's lamp alongside him. Every shadow on the black, dusty walls could be the last thing we see!"

Charlie would lower his voice to a scary-sounding whisper.

"Because, just when you think everything's safe, some deadly gases might be coming back up the tunnel towards you. You can't see them. You can't smell them or taste them. The first thing you would know about is ... BOOM!"

Charlie would roar out the last word, and I would almost fall off my chair in fright.

"It's my father's job to locate any dangerous gases in the tunnels," Charlie would continue. "He keeps a careful watch on the flame of his own oil lamp. Every few minutes, we stop. 'Watch out, Charlie,' he says. 'Here we go!'"

"My father slowly raises his arm, and lifts the oil lamp higher and higher. Our eyes are fixed on the flame. We hold our breath. If the flame starts to grow, and sputters and spits brightly, we know there are gases gathering up by that part of the roof. 'Gas!' he warns. 'Write a warning, Charlie!'"

"Then, I grab this," continued Charlie, holding a white lump of chalk. "And then I find the nearest shovel. I write this warning on the shovel, and I rest it up against the wall."

"Beware Of Gas!" read the warning. Then Charlie would write the date, in big curving numbers underneath. Charlie would also scrawl the warning on the nearby walls too.

"The next morning, all the miners see my warning messages. They'll know where to be extra careful with flames and lamps."

I was envious of Charlie — his life was much more exciting than mine. I wished I had a job creeping and crawling through tunnels surrounded by dangerous gases and warnings. But I knew my father would never allow it. One day, I would have to sit next to him in his office. The most exciting thing in my day would be adding up columns and rows of numbers in large, leather-bound accounts books.

"You're so lucky, Charlie," I would say.

"So far," Charlie would reply. "So far!"

Chapter 2.

That night, after I watched Charlie and his father whistling their way towards Blackwater Mine, I felt bored and cold so I went downstairs to warm myself by the fire.

My mother was reading a book by candlelight, and gently turning each page as she finished it. My father was reading his newspaper a lot less gently. He read a story that really put him in a black mood.

"Davy Lamps!" he snorted. "The mine owners up north have started giving their miners some sort of safety lamp called a Davy Lamp."

He glared at my mother, knowing that she would be on the miners' side.

"Next thing you know, the miners here will want one, too. This fellow Davy will ruin my business. How will I be able to afford a hundred Davy Lamps?"

"How do they work?" I asked. My father slowly read out the words that had infuriated him.

"A tiny net of wires covers the flame," he began. "The wires cool the flame, so it is cooler than the temperature required to explode gases. What nonsense," he said scornfully. "Whoever heard of a cool flame?"

"Besides," he said, rustling his newspaper angrily. "That's what I pay that fellow Grimes and his son for. I pay them to check my mine every night. If they can't check it properly, *they* should pay for a hundred Davy Lamps."

My thoughts switched to Charlie and his father, crawling along on their hands and knees in the inky blackness of our mine, at this very moment. For a few pennies, they risked their lives to warn the other miners of danger.
I was sure that Charlie's mother would think they were worth the cost of a hundred Davy Lamps. But my father would take more convincing.

The next day, when I sneaked out of the house to meet with Charlie, I was eager to tell him about the new Davy Lamp. How would he react? Would he be pleased to hear that it might soon be safer to work in dangerous coal mines? Or would he be concerned that his job, and that of his father, might soon disappear?

I crept through the paddock behind our house, and as soon as I saw Charlie, I knew something was wrong. His family couldn't afford newspapers, so it couldn't be the new invention he was worried about. I asked what was wrong.

"It's my father," he said glumly. "Coal dust in his lungs. He's been coughing badly for the last couple of days. Today he can hardly breathe. He's afraid he won't be able to work tonight."

I was concerned for Charlie and his father. Coal dust could make you very, very ill. It was common to see old miners, coughing and spluttering their way along the village streets.

Even though they might have only been young men, they looked like blackened, wrinkled old men. It was horrible to see hard-working men hunched over and spitting out black poison when the coughing became too much for them. Worse still, I knew that my father would have no sympathy for Charlie's father. All he would do was complain about who would do his job.

"What will you do?" I asked Charlie.

He looked at me, and sat tall on the log we were sharing.

"I'm ten years old. I'm old enough to do the job," he replied in a grown-up voice. "Lots of boys have been working for years when they're as old as I am. I've seen my father do the job a hundred times. Tonight, I will do it myself."

I stared at Charlie in disbelief. He was going to go down Blackwater Mine, checking for dangerous gases in the dead of night, alone?

"But you can't!" I protested. "What if something happens?"

"Like you said, Nat, I've been lucky so far. Besides," he added, "we need the money. If we don't get paid, we don't eat."

Suddenly, I had a daring thought that filled me with dread and excitement, all at the same time. I grabbed Charlie's arm, and whispered excitedly.

"Charlie!" I hissed. "I'll come with you!"

Chapter 3.

Charlie looked at me as if I was mad. The son of the mine owner, crawling along in the damp, dusty gas-filled tunnels? It was absolute madness!

"Leave a little later than usual," I said, trying to convince Charlie that I had a good plan. "Wait until midnight. My father and mother will have been asleep for hours. I'll creep outside, and meet you. Then you can do your father's job, and I'll do yours!"

A cloud of worry crossed Charlie's dark face. But I pressed him harder to agree with me.

"Give me the chalk, Charlie. I can do it!" I pleaded.

Reluctantly, Charlie scrabbled around in his pocket, and handed over the lump of creamy chalk that he always carried. Our plan was set. Tonight would be a night of danger and adventure. I could hardly wait.

That evening, the minutes seemed to stretch out forever. I sat patiently, pretending to read a book, and wishing my mother and father would go to bed. At last, my father yawned, and rubbed his forehead. He drew out a gleaming gold pocket watch.

"Eight o'clock," he declared. Just then, the grandfather clock in the drawing room started to chime in agreement. My mother and I knew that he hated burning lamp oil and candles past eight o'clock. It was 'money going up in smoke', he would say. My mother carefully marked the page of her book with a delicately embroidered bookmark.

Quickly, I stood up and yawned. I said goodnight, and went upstairs. But sleep was the last thing on my mind!

As I lay in bed, all I could think of was my job in the mine that night. With each chime of the grandfather clock, I became more excited. Nine o'clock. Ten o'clock. Eleven o'clock. At the first stroke of twelve, I leapt out of bed.

Silently and quickly I got dressed in the oldest clothes I could find. I crept down the stairs, carefully avoiding any creaky floorboards. Gently I lifted the heavy brass latch on the front door. Then I was out, running swiftly across the paddock towards the secret meeting place.

"Charlie!" I hissed. "Charlie, are you there?"

A hand shot out of the darkness and grabbed my shoulder. I whirled around to see two bright eyes and a row of white teeth grinning at me in the moonlight.

"Let's get to work," he said, leading me towards the entrance to the mine. When he started to whistle, I joined in.

When we reached the mouth of the mine, I felt another wave of excitement. I wasn't scared. For the first time, I was doing something really important to help a friend. It also meant going somewhere forbidden by my father. I had never been allowed to set foot inside the mine. Once or twice, I had asked my father, but his answer was always the same.

"Inside a mine is no place for a child of mine," my father would answer sternly. "Our place is up here," he would add, "up here, in charge of everyone else."

Charlie knelt down at the mine's entrance. He lit his father's oil lamp, and a deep orange glow lit our surroundings. His face was silhouetted by the light of its tiny flame. With a deep breath of fresh air, I followed him inside the mine.

A twin row of rail tracks lay beneath us, disappearing into the inky darkness ahead. I could see that the miners had curved old pieces of rail track to make supports for the roof.

Here and there, gigantic beams of wood added further strength. The walls were black and damp. Shovels and picks lined the walls, as we crept deeper and deeper into the black earth.

Suddenly, Charlie crouched down. He cupped the flame of his lamp with one hand and turned to me. He looked very serious.

"From here on, we crawl," he instructed. "Watch out, Nat," he added. "Here we go!"

A feeling of terror gripped me for the first time. I imagined a huge, deadly swirling mist of explosive gases, rushing up to greet us. But I couldn't let Charlie know I felt scared.

I fumbled for my piece of chalk, and held it tightly. On hands and knees, I followed him, deeper and deeper into the blackness.

Silently, Charlie raised his hand. I stopped instantly. Cautiously, he lifted his lamp higher. My eyes fixed on the flame. Was the deadly gas waiting for us? Would the flame sputter and burn brighter? But nothing happened. The flame burned without a flicker in the motionless, cold air.

Charlie lowered the lamp, and crept onwards. I followed behind, taking in short breaths of dirty air. The damp from the floor of the mine started to seep through the knees and elbows of my clothes. The smell of the coal dust clogging my nose and throat was sharp and bitter. We crawled for ages, until Charlie raised his hand again. My heart thumped as he slowly raised the lamp.

Again, nothing. I breathed a sigh of relief. How could Charlie and his father feel this tension, night after night?

I shivered in the cold, damp air. They deserved every penny they got for doing this job.

Once more, Charlie lowered the lamp. We headed down a steep incline. The cold steel of the rails pressed into the sides of my legs, as we moved further and further into the depths of the mine.

Charlie stopped. All I could see was his shadow in front of me, and the weird glow of his lamp, lighting a small hazy circle around us. The coal dust in the air was now choking me. I coughed, and drew in a great lungful of the thick, dirty air.

"Watch out, Nat," Charlie whispered.

I watched as he rose the lamp for a third time. With a cold feeling of horror, I saw it flicker and turn from orange to bright white.

"Charlie!" I yelled.

In a split-second, a luminous blue sheet of flame burst along the roof of the mine, and the rest of my warning was swept away in a terrific whoosh of flaming gas.

Instantly, the cool, motionless air became a sucking, turbulent gale, as the blinding flame rippled like a deadly burning blanket above us.

"Get down!" I heard Charlie yell. I dropped to my stomach and pressed myself into the filthy coal floor, arms desperately trying to cover my head. The flame poured along the mine roof at terrifying speed, feeding on the air and gas mixture that was being sucked up from the deep. With a boom like cannon fire, it burst out the mouth of the mine.

The tremendous explosion shook the earth. Somewhere, behind us, there was a scary cracking sound.

Then, just as suddenly as it had started, the sheet of flame died. Blackness enveloped us again, and the silence was almost as deafening as the explosion. A wave of coal dust swept over us, like a choking, thick fog. Charlie's lamp blew out. I had a disgusting, rotten taste in my mouth. My nose and eyes stung. Something kicked my arms urgently.

“Go back!” Charlie yelled. His voice was shaking. “Go back! Now!”

At least we were both alive, I thought. Knowing that, the only other thing I could think of was getting out of the mine, back into the clean night air. I wanted to see the moon and the stars, instead of this inky blackness.

I inched my way backwards, coughing and spitting. The air seemed as thick as mud. I blindly felt my way along the rails. It couldn’t be that far, I thought to myself. Soon, we would breathe the cool, night air. I kept moving backwards. I could see nothing. Charlie was urging me on. Then, in confusion, I felt something hard behind me. I groped around. My fingers scrabbled amongst lumps of hard, jagged coal. Where was the way out? The tracks seemed to stop in the middle of this pile of coal. I tried to feel my way past, but the tunnel had disappeared.

I realised with a sinking feeling that the mine roof had collapsed. We were trapped!

Chapter 4.

Thoughts panicked in my mind. "Charlie," I coughed. My voice seemed strangely muffled. "We're trapped!"

Charlie was strangely silent. I hoped he was thinking of some way out. But, when Charlie couldn't think of anything, my hopes faded. Both Charlie and I knew what happened to miners trapped by a collapsed mine roof. Unless someone dug their way through to rescue them quickly, they usually stayed trapped — forever!

Charlie and I huddled together, wondering how long it would be before the air in the blocked tunnel ran out. Although I could not see him, it was comforting to know that I was not alone. He started to whistle, a low, mournful whistle, and I joined in. If anyone could have heard us, it must have sounded like a dreadfully slow, sad tune.

Little did we know, but at that very moment, the entrance to the mine was as busy as a beehive. The explosion had woken the entire village. Everyone had rushed down to Blackwater Mine to find out what had happened.

At the head of the group of anxious, determined miners, feverishly digging away at the coal fall, was my father. He had rushed in to my room to check on me before he left but, of course, I was nowhere to be found. When he had seen Charlie's father staggering towards the mine, coughing and spluttering, a wave of relief had washed over him. At least, he thought, there was no-one down in the mine.

But when Charlie's father explained that his son had gone down into the mine to check the gases instead of him, both fathers had the same terrifying thought at once. Charlie would never have gone to work alone — and I was missing. It could only mean one thing.

Digging away at the caved-in entrance to the mine was urgent work. No-one knew what they would find. Were we alive? But, for the first time at Blackwater Mine, the mine owner and his miners worked side by side, tirelessly digging and hauling away tonnes of coal. For hours they dug, feeling dread, but also hope. Finally, they broke through.

We must have looked like two dirty rag dolls, dangling exhausted in the arms of the miners. Everyone said there was a great cheer from the villagers as they saw the miners rush our two, tired bodies out into the night air.

But all Charlie and I could remember was the relief on our father's faces, before exhaustion set in. The darkness was slowly replaced by a deep, dreamless sleep. The next thing I can remember is waking up in my house, in bed, surrounded by a sea of worried faces.

My father was furious with me and Charlie. But there was also concern in his voice. He had never expected to see his son rescued from a deep, dangerous mine. The experience of knowing what it felt like to have one of your own family trapped in a deadly situation changed him. In those long, desperate hours, he gained some small understanding of what it must feel like to belong to a miner's family.

In the following weeks, he arranged to buy each miner a Davy Lamp. And there were never any more complaints about how expensive safety was. Whenever some better equipment was invented, he quietly bought it, and Blackwater Mine became safer and safer.

Epilogue

Fifty years later, Blackwater Mine is the safest mine in the country, but we are always watchful for any dangers. As mine owner, it is now my responsibility, and I take it seriously. One of the first changes I made in Blackwater Mine was to ban boys from working in the mine until they were 18 years old. I know exactly what it feels like to be trapped in a deadly situation, and I didn't want a repeat accident to happen.

And, you may ask, whatever happened to Charlie?

As I glance up from my desk, I can peer through the tinted glass window, into the office next door. There, he sits, Mr Charles Grimes. The sign on his desk reads 'Mine Manager'. You could say that the night of the Blackwater Mine disaster was our first night working together: and we've been working together ever since. Sometimes, at the end of a long day, I'll hear a familiar sound coming from his office: Charlie whistling, happy to be alive.

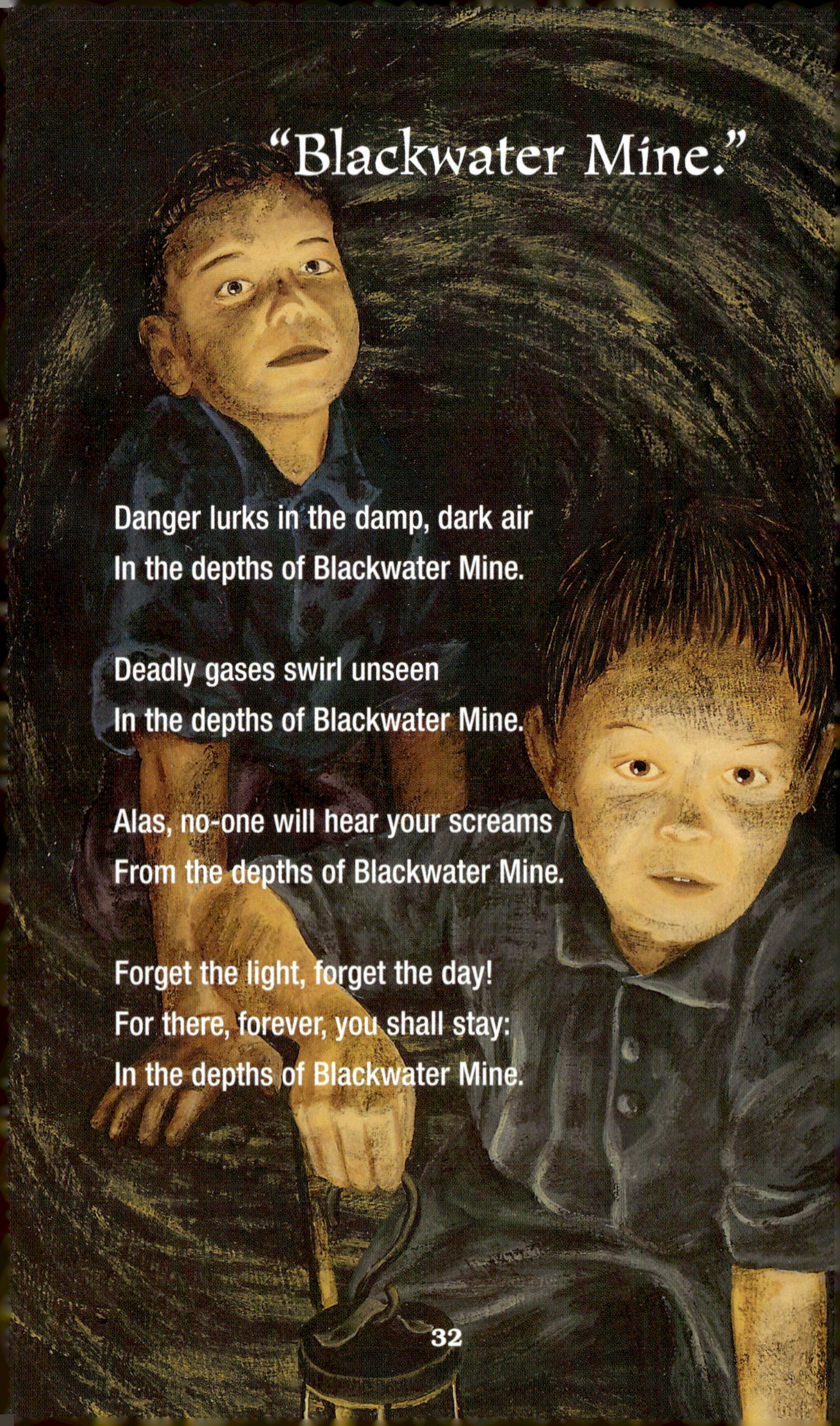

"Blackwater Mine."

Danger lurks in the damp, dark air
In the depths of Blackwater Mine.

Deadly gases swirl unseen
In the depths of Blackwater Mine.

Alas, no-one will hear your screams
From the depths of Blackwater Mine.

Forget the light, forget the day!
For there, forever, you shall stay:
In the depths of Blackwater Mine.